WEIGHT T
FOR MEN

Tony Lycholat

THORSONS PUBLISHING GROUP
Wellingborough, Northamptonshire
Rochester, Vermont

First published April 1985
Second Impression
November 1985
Third Impression
July 1986

© THORSONS PUBLISHING
GROUP LIMITED 1985

Photography
  Philip Yarde

Cover photography
  Barry A. Payling

Printed and bound in
Great Britain

British Library Cataloguing in
Publication Data:

Lycholat, Tony
  Weight training for men.
  1. Weight lifting
  1. Title
  796.4'1   GV546.5
  ISBN 0-7225-1178-7

SPECIAL NOTE

As with any exercise programme,
you should consult your doctor
before you start. If you have any
special problems, such as being
overweight, diabetic or if you suffer
from a specific illness, or drink or
smoke heavily, you should discuss
plans fully with your doctor before
you start.

Contents

INTRODUCTION

First of all, let's get a problem of words out of the way! Many people are confused by the term "weight training", often wrongly using it instead of the words "weight lifting" or "body building".

"Weight training" refers to exercising with weights to aid the development of certain components of fitness, either as an end in themselves, or to improve performance in a particular sport or activity. "Weight lifting" refers to a competitive activity recognised by the Olympic Movement which is all about trying to lift the heaviest possible weight above one's head. "Body building" refers to a competitive activity which is geared to obtaining maximum muscular development (size and symmetry) through the use of weights. Body building is exemplified by the "Mr Universe" contests. It is with the use of weights to develop the benefits of health, fitness and well-being that this book is concerned.

Secondly, there are a number of popular myths surrounding weight training for men which must be dispelled.

● **"Muscle turns to fat on cessation of exercise"**
Muscle and fat are different tissues and you cannot change one to the other, although you can change their relative proportions. Appropriate exercise can lead to an increase in muscle mass and a decrease in fat mass: one has not changed into the other, one has just become more and the other less.

● **"Weight training makes you 'muscle bound'"**
A well constructed and executed weight training programme does not lead to a decrease in flexibility – quite the reverse. Excessive muscular development can be a limiting factor in movement at a joint however, since the muscle bulk "gets in the way" of normal joint movement.

● "Men who exercise with weights end up with bulging muscles"

Whether any individual develops muscle bulk as a result of weight training depends upon the type of programme being followed and the individual: stocky people tend to put on muscle bulk easily. The programme outlined in this book, if followed correctly, will lead to a finer more defined shape without bulk.

● "Training with weights causes excessive muscle soreness"

If you follow the programme accurately, never omitting to warm up and cool down, you should experience few problems. Some stiffness following exercise is acceptable, acute soreness is not. If this soreness appears some time after exercise, it means you have done too much. Certainly if you are so sore that you cannot exercise two days later your initial exercise bout was too intense. Return to exercise as soon as you feel able and cut back on the amount of exercise you do. If your problem occurred during exercise, you have injured something so seek specialist advice. : Remember it is better to do too little than too much too soon.

A well constructed and executed weight training programme offers men an exciting list of potential benefits; these are some of them:

- Increased muscular strength

- Increased muscular endurance

- Increased stamina

- Increased flexibility and mobility

- Stronger and more injury resistant joints

- A decrease in body fat

- Improved posture

- Improved shape

- Improved coordination

- An increased ability to carry out daily tasks

- An increase in one's general sense of well-being

- A decrease in harmful stress

- An increase in self-confidence

- An improvement in one's social life

These are good reasons for embarking upon a weight training programme, because if you put all the benefits together you will see that they make you fit for life in general ... but the benefits can only occur with a well constructed and executed weight training programme. It now follows!

Tony Lycholat

What is Physical Fitness?

There is no one single definition of fitness precisely because the concept of fitness is individually specific and has many components. A very general definition would read something like: "being able to do what you want to do, when you want to do it", and this would be as true for the man in the street as it would be for Daley Thompson. Yet this neglects to indicate that there are tremendous health gains associated with regular exercise both mental and physical.

The object of any exercise programme should be to aid the development of as many of the components of physical fitness as possible which will also influence health and well-being, whilst at the same time bearing in mind the needs and requirements of the individual.

Components of Physical Fitness

Muscular Strength

Strength basically refers to the amount of force a muscle or muscle group can produce, and maximum strength is the greatest amount of force a muscle or muscle group can produce in a single voluntary contraction. In everyday activities strength is important if we wish to lift something heavy off the floor.

Muscular Endurance

If a muscle can repeatedly perform the same task, withstanding fatigue, it is said to have a high degree of muscular endurance. The importance of muscular endurance is evident in everyday activities which you have to do repeatedly.

Power

Power brings into account the element of speed. Someone can be said to be powerful if they can lift something heavy off the floor quickly, for instance. Hence power is an expression of muscular strength and speed.

Flexibility

Flexibility refers to range of movement at a joint. In everyday life, if someone is flexible they will find it easier to reach, bend and twist. Coupled with strength it allows for the safe execution of many activities and leads to a greater freedom of movement.

Stamina

Stamina reflects muscular endurance throughout the body and requires that the muscles be "backed-up" by an efficient heart, lungs, and circulatory system: of extreme importance in performing "whole body" tasks such as walking, jogging, cycling, swimming.

Other components of fitness which are subsidiary to these include skill, agility and coordination which involve timing and changes in bodily movement coupled with proficiency in any given tasks. Yet fitness is not just physical, for psychological fitness is as important in the goal of being fit for life, and healthy.

Fortunately exercise, providing it is suited to the individual, can act as a catalyst for the improvement of mental health and social awareness.

Theory of Exercising with Weights

Hippocrates said it first: "That which is used develops, that which is not wastes away." Our bodies are designed for action, unfortunately contemporary lifestyle is not. Most of us spend far too much time doing very little of a physical nature with the result being a loss in physical, and often mental, efficiency. To restore our bodies to their efficient best we need to do more work than we do normally, that is we must overload a system or systems of the body just enough so that the system adapts. Essentially the body sees exercise as just another threat to its everyday functioning and in the face of the threat of exercise, the body adapts in the long term such that the exercise no longer exists as that threat. For example in the case of lifting a very heavy weight up and down, the muscles engaged in the action become stronger and more capable of performing the required action.

This sequence of events holds true for all the components of fitness, remembering that exercise is specific, hence you get what you train for.

It is therefore necessary to judge the nature of the overload accurately. If we just wanted maximum strength we would need to train by lifting very heavy weights up and down just a few times. Conversely if we just wanted muscular endurance we would need to train by lifting light weights up and down many times. Training for power would require lifting heavy weights up and down as rapidly as possible. Yet for general fitness we do not want the extremes: we need some of each.

Hence a good general programme involves lifting a given weight 12-15 times. That weight would be heavy enough such that only 12-15 repetitions (number of lifts) can be performed. If you cannot raise and lower the weight that number of times, it is too heavy; if you can lift it more times than this it is too light. The total number of repetitions performed in one go constitutes a set.

The beauty of using weights is that you can work at a level which is suitable for you: you do not have to work with the same weight as a friend. Because of this, weight training can most accurately be suited to your current level of fitness and the weights can be increased as your fitness level increases.

Self Assessment

Before embarking upon any exercise regime, ask yourself a few questions:

Am I extremely overweight?

Do I have any joint or muscle problems?

Do I have high blood pressure or any cardiac or circulatory problem?

Am I prone to dizziness or fainting spells?

Am I taking drugs or medication?

Do I become breathless or dizzy upon slight exertion?

If your answer is yes to any of these questions or if you have any doubts as to your suitability for a weight training programme seek advice from an exercise physiologist or doctor. Certainly if you are in doubt or are over 35 years old you are advised to seek specialist advice including medical screening and an exercise stress test.

If when you exercise you experience any problems, e.g. feeling faint, nauseous, dizzy, chest pain, etc. also seek medical advice.

Always be health and safety conscious and listen to your body. If you do not understand what your body is telling you, find a specialist who does.

What to Wear

You will be putting yourself into positions you have not been in for a long time! Make sure you can move easily and comfortably. Most men tend to exercise in T shirts and shorts with a track suit over the top. This is useful since as you get warmer you can take the track suit off, replacing it at the end of the session. However, some gyms prefer you to wear a track suit at all times to prevent you from sweating over the equipment.

Good shoes are a must for weight training. Squash type or aerobics shoes are very popular, and more suitable than running shoes.

Designing your Programme

Weight training, or any exercise for that matter, *must* be preceded by warming-up activities.

A warm-up phase serves the purpose of preparing the body for more strenuous activity and should be designed with 2 things in mind. Firstly, all the joints and muscles of the body need to be mobilised. This should be done by gradually increasing the range and intensity of the movements employed. All movements in a warm-up phase should be rhythmical and controlled, never jerky. By working in this manner you are less likely to injure yourself when you begin exercising in earnest.

The body also functions more efficiently with an increase in temperature, so your warm-up phase must also include large muscle group activities which generate body heat such as jogging, skipping or stationary cycling in the gym or home. With mobilising work and large muscle group activities your warm-up phase should last 10-15 minutes. Older or more unfit individuals should spend a longer time warming-up, approximately 15-20 minutes.

The exercise section of the book is divided into sections for different parts of the body. In general you need one or two exercises for each body part, so that your programme consists of 10-12 weight-training exercises. However, this is fairly flexible since if you feel you need more work on a certain area of the body you can include more exercises for this region. Always balance your programme as much as possible though and do not neglect any region of the body altogether.

There is a certain amount of skill learning involved in any new exercise regime and it is best and safest to perform all your exercises to begin with using light weights, or no weights at all. It is crucial to exercise technically correctly, and you should *never sacrifice technique just to lift heavier weights.* Only when you have mastered the technique of an exercise should you increase the weight you are using. If your technique deteriorates with the use of a new, heavier weight, that weight is too heavy so return to a lighter weight.

Because this is a book geared to improving overall fitness you should aim to do each exercise 12-15 times, that is, 12-15 repetitions. Do not worry if you cannot manage that many to begin with, after a few sessions you will find it becomes easier. Always do as many as you can manage comfortably and try and add on repetitions as you become more proficient until you reach your target of 12-15.

Move swiftly from one exercise to the next, in this manner you will increase your stamina.

When you can do all the exercises in your programme the required number of times fairly easily, choose 4-6 exercises in your programme and repeat them. That is, do 2 *sets* of 12-15 repetitions of these exercises. Eventually work up to do 2 sets of 12-15 repetitions on each exercise. Aim to complete 3 sets of all the exercises in your programme progressively as outlined, as the weeks go by.

When this becomes easy indicating your improved fitness level you have several options open to you:

● Substitute exercises for some of the other exercises in the same section.

● Add more exercises to your programme.

● Increase the weights on some of your exercises gradually, until you have increased the weights on all of them.

As you can see, the tremendous choice offered by weight-training makes it interesting and varied, and because you can measure progress and see change the stimulus for continued participation is always there.

Always make a record of your programme: the exercises, number of sets and repetitions and the weight. It is good to look back on as the weeks go by.

● Always make sure that at the end of your exercise bout you cool down thoroughly, i.e. make sure you bring yourself back to normal at the end of the session. Cooling down activities can involve stretching, light rhythmical work and light all-body activities which gradually decrease in intensity to return to the resting state.

Cooling down is vitally important and should not be dismissed since this phase allows the body to recover far more quickly, and prevents muscle soreness to a large extent.

To obtain maximum benefit from an exercise programme it must be carried out on a regular basis, preferably 3 times a week at equally spaced intervals, approximately once every 2 days. Certainly a day between exercise bouts gives your body a chance to recover.

Safety

A Summary of Programme Safety

● Always warm-up thoroughly, gradually increasing the range and intensity of movement.

● Always balance your programme.

● Only increase weights and/or repetitions when you have mastered technique and are fit enough to do so.

● Aim to do each exercise 12-15 times.

● Move swiftly from one exercise to the next.

● Work progressively, eventually aiming to do 3 sets of 12-15 repetitions on all your exercises.

● Vary your programme to prevent boredom.

● Record your programme.

● Exercise 3 times a week at evenly spaced intervals.

● Always cool down thoroughly.

● Work at your speed and listen to your body.

Safety Rules for You

● Always observe correct technique in all exercises.

● When lifting weights off the floor, always bend your knees and keep your back flat. You must use your legs to lift the weights up, and equally important, to put weights down again. This applies to all exercises performed in a standing position, or involving lifting and lowering any weight from the floor.

● Always exercise from a firm base. You should feel stable and balanced.

● Never train or exercise if you feel unwell, have a cold or virus, or have just eaten a heavy meal.

● Always remember to breathe. Never hold your breath.

Equipment Safety Rules

● Make sure you are dressed appropriately.

● Always check equipment before you use it. Make sure collars are on and tightened, pins are in the right place, the equipment has been adjusted for your use, benches are stable.

● When using dumbbells or barbells make sure they have an equal amount of weight on each end.

● If you add or remove weights to or from a bar, make sure it is on the floor.

● Always train with a partner. This is especially important when performing movements overhead with free weights in an awkward position, e.g. Squats, Bench press.

● When using a barbell make sure it moves in a parallel manner: do not let it wobble.

● Execute all movements smoothly without jerking. You should be in control of the weight and not the other way round.

Equipment Explained

In many exercises the weight of the limbs or body can be used most effectively as the necessary overload required to obtain a training effect. When this is not possible or impractical weights can be held in the hands, or strapped on to the wrists or ankles.

A *dumbbell* is simply a short rod fitted with a weight at either end. The simplest versions allow you to add discs of various weights to each end securing them with collars which have screw fastenings. More modern versions are often in set weights finished in chrome ranging from 1 Kg to 50 Kg.

A *barbell* is a much longer rod to which weights can be fitted at either end in the same manner as a dumbbell. These too can appear in chromed sets.

Barbells are used in activities involving symmetrical actions needing two hands, dumbbells are used for one hand work. Strap on ankle or wrist weights also come in a variety of weight sizes and are useful particularly for leg and buttock work.

Some exercises require more elaborate equipment. At the simplest level equipment exists to which you just add weight discs. Other basic equipment includes pulleys so that pulling, rather than just pushing and pressing movements can be carried out.

A step up from this level, equipment exists which incorporates a stack of weights in its design. Altering the weight you are using on equipment like this is made very simple since you just change the position of a pin in the weight being handled. Another advantage of this type of equipment is that it does not matter if you get into difficulties since the weights move along runners and cannot drop or fall on you (example Powersport

Multigym). In a multigym arrangement a number of exercise stations are grouped together in one central block (see illustration) allowing you to work round it easily and quickly, although single station exercise machines are more popular.

Other equipment exists which incorporates a weight stack and a cam (e.g. Nautilus) or offset sphere (e.g. Atlanta). These methods allow the resistance you are overcoming to alter with the change in mechanical advantage and force you can apply as you perform any movement. In other words you can condition a muscle more effectively throughout its full range. This type of equipment is often very visually appealing and comfortable.

Yet for all round development it is best to use a variety of equipment: free weights, standard multigym type apparatus and variable resistance apparatus, such as Nautilus or Atlanta. No one system gives you everything.

The exercises described here use a minimum of equipment and many can be done in the home or basic gymnasium. For some exercises more elaborate and expensive equipment is necessary, which will only be found in a well equipped gym, or health club.

Although this book gives accurate instructions do seek advice from an instructor if you have problems.

Warm Ups

Your warm up should last 10-15 minutes. Older and more unfit individuals should spend 15-20 minutes on this phase.

POSTURE

It is always a good idea to check your posture prior to exercise since exercising with poor posture only exacerbates your faults, and may lead to injury. Your feet should be a comfortable distance apart, about hip width, with your weight evenly balanced. Your shoulders should be down away from your ears and you should be looking forward. Your spine should feel lengthened from your tail right up to your head.

SHOULDER CIRCLES

Having adjusted your posture, place your feet slightly wider apart to give you a more stable base. Keeping your arms down, lift your shoulders up towards your ears, then press them backwards, finally bringing them back to their resting position. Breathe comfortably throughout.

Repeat 12 times.

ARM CIRCLES

Standing in the same position as in the previous exercise, take one arm backwards in a giant circle. Your body should not move since the action takes places only at the shoulder joint. Your upper arm should brush your ear.

Breathe comfortably throughout.

Repeat 12 times on each side.

HIP CIRCLES

Stand tall as before with your feet spaced more widely apart. With your hands on hips, smoothly swing your hips to the side, round to the back, to the other side and finally forward in a large circle.

This is not a jerky movement.

Remember to breathe regularly throughout.

Repeat 12 times in either direction.

WAIST TWISTS

Standing with feet apart and knees slightly bent twist your upper body smoothly round as far as possible without jerking making sure that your hips remain facing forward. You should still have that feeling of length in the spine, with your shoulders relaxed.

Breathe easily throughout.

Repeat 12 times in each direction.

SIDE BENDS

Stand tall with feet apart. Smoothly bend to the side making sure you do not bend either forwards or backwards.You should have a feeling of lifting up and over to the side, not one of collapsing!

Breathe out as you bend to the side, in as you return.

Repeat 12 times on each side.

LEG SWINGS

Stand tall, sideways on to a chair, resting the fingers of one hand lightly on the chair for balance – it is not there to hold you up. Rest your other hand on your hip. Freely swing your outside leg forward and backward without jerking. This is a nice rhythmical flowing movement.

Breathe easily throughout.

Turn to face the other side and repeat 12 times for each leg.

KNEES TO CHEST

Stand tall. Maintain your upright stance as you bring one knee upwards to meet the elbow of the opposite arm. Repeat on the other side. Breathe easily throughout and repeat whole sequence 12 times on each side.

30

FORWARD LUNGE

Stand with one leg forward and one leg back but maintaining the feeling of lengthening in the spine. Your feet should be parallel and hip width apart, hands resting on hips.

Bend the knee of the leading leg so that it moves to a position approximately over the toe. Make sure that your knee stays in line with your foot.

The back leg should remain straight. (An added bonus can be gained from this exercise if the heel of the foot of the back leg is pressed into the floor giving a stretch of the calf.)

Return to the starting position, repeating 12 times on each leg.

Breathe easily throughout.

JOGGING

When jogging, as in the standing exercises, it is important to "think tall". In this case run tall. Make sure you use the whole of the foot ensuring that your heels always come down, particularly if you are running on the spot. Jogging should be a relaxed, easy movement sequence: there should be no untoward tension in the neck, shoulders, arms or hands.

CYCLING

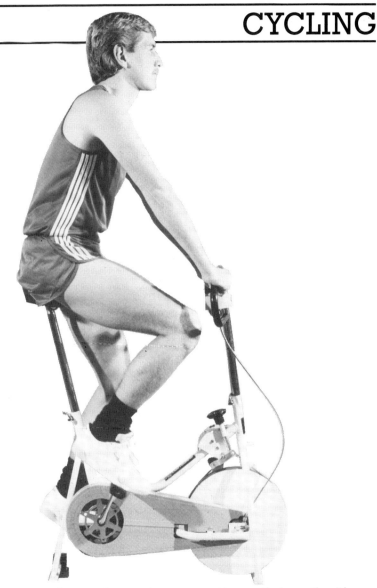

Many men prefer to cycle on a stationary bicycle in the gym or home as part of their warm up phase. If this appeals to you always make sure you have adjusted the seat height correctly, so that on the "downstroke" the leg is almost fully extended. A comfortable cycling speed is one of 50-60 revolutions of the crank per minute.

HALF SQUATS

For the muscles of the legs and those around the hips and buttocks.

Stand tall with your feet hip width to shoulder width apart with a bar or light barbell sitting comfortably across the shoulders/upper back. Hold the bar firmly with a wide grip.

Keeping your back flat throughout and your head in the same line as your spine, bend your knees, controlling your movement down. (It is neither necessary nor advisable to go down to a position lower than that illustrated to begin with. In general the lowest position you should attempt is one where your thighs are parallel to the ground.)

Return smoothly to your starting position making sure you fully straighten the legs.

If you feel unstable because your heels leave the floor as you squat, stand with your heels on a block of wood – approx. 1″ high.

Breathe in as you descend, out as you rise.

Always make sure your knees follow the same line as your toes.

The machine version of this exercise is on either a leg press or duo squat machine.

THIGH EXTENSION

For the front thigh muscles.

This exercise can only be done most effectively and comfortably on a purpose built thigh extension machine. Sit on the seat or bench. If the machine has a back rest make sure your back is pressed into it, if there is no back rest use your arms behind you to keep stable and upright. You should be positioned so that the backs of your knees are resting comfortably on the edge of the bench with your feet hooked under the padded roller.

Smoothly straighten your legs so that they are fully extended. Hold this position then lower smoothly to the starting position, and just as the weights touch, repeat the sequence.

Breathe comfortably throughout and keep the rest of your body as relaxed as possible.

LEG CURL

(not illustrated)

For the muscles at the back of the thighs.

Lie face down on the bench with the front of your knees just off the edge of the bench and the backs of your ankles under the padded roller.

Making sure that your hips remain firmly pressed into the bench and your upper body is relaxed, attempt to bring your heels to touch your buttocks, without jerking, then smoothly lower to the starting position. Just as soon as the weights touch, repeat the sequence.

Breathe comfortably throughout.

HEEL RAISE

For the muscles of the calf.

Assume the starting position as for the half squat with a bar or light barbell resting across the shoulders/ upper back. Then stand with the balls of your feet resting on a block of wood (or telephone directory), heels on the floor. Your legs should be straight. From this position, rise up on to your toes, hold momentarily, returning to the starting position and repeating the sequence.

Breathe easily throughout.

37

SIDE LEG LIFTS

For muscles on the outside of hip and thigh.

Use no weights or light ankle weights to begin with.

Lie on your side so that you have a straight line from ankle, knee, hip and shoulder. Rest your head on your lower arm and use your top arm as a support in front of your body.

Keep your hips facing forward and smoothly raise your top leg, ensuring that the knee and foot of this leg always face forward. Avoid the tendency to roll forwards or backwards.

Hold your uppermost position momentarily, then slowly lower to the starting position.

Repeat on other side.

Breathe easily throughout.

These muscles can be very effectively conditioned using any hip abductor machine.

LOWER LEG LIFTS

For the muscles of the inner thigh.

Use no weights, or light ankle weights to begin with.

Assume the side lying position as in the previous exercise. This time, however, bring the top leg over and forward of the lower leg.

Making sure that the hips are facing forward, lift the lower leg off the floor as high as possible.

Keep the knee and foot of this leg also facing forward.

Hold the top position momentarily then slowly lower.

Just as the ankle touches the floor, repeat the sequence.

Repeat on both sides, breathing easily throughout.

These muscles can be very effectively conditioned using any hip adductor machine.

ARM CURL

For the muscles of the front of the upper arm.

Stand tall, feet shoulder width apart. Grip a barbell with palms facing forward, hands slightly wider than hip width apart. Keeping your upright position with upper arms remaining close to the sides of the body, bend your arms at the elbow, smoothly bringing the bar to meet the chest. Note that the upper arm remains in its fixed starting position and the movement takes place solely about the elbow joint.

Smoothly return the bar to the starting position and repeat.

Make sure you work through the full range of movement and avoid the tendency to lean forward or backward when lifting and lowering the bar.

Breathe in as you raise the bar and out as you lower it.

ALTERNATE DUMBBELL CURL

For the muscles at the front of the upper arm.

The starting position is the same as for the previous exercise except you are holding a dumbbell in either hand, palms facing your sides, at arm's length. Keeping the upper arm close to the body and standing tall throughout, bend one arm at the elbow to bring the dumbbell to your shoulder, twisting the dumbbell through ninety degrees as you do so.

Smoothly return this dumbbell to its starting position and repeat on the other side. As before, breathe in as you raise each weight and out as you lower.

41

SEATED TRICEP PRESS

For the muscles at the back of the upper arm.

Sit upright on a bench or sturdy chair. Place your feet apart and flat on the floor to give a firm stable base.

Hold a dumbbell in one hand with the upper arm vertical, close to the head and flexed at the elbow.

Smoothly straighten this arm at the elbow, keeping the upper arm in exactly the same position at all times, then control the movement back to the starting position.

Repeat the sequence on both sides.

Breathe in as you raise the weight and out as you lower it.

SEATED PRESS BEHIND NECK

For the muscles of the shoulder, backs of upper arms, upper back.

Place a bar or light barbell across your shoulders as for the half squat exercise: or get a partner to help you. Then sit upright on a bench or sturdy chair.

Smoothly press the barbell upward so it ends up at arm's length overhead. Return the barbell under control until it just touches the neck then repeat the sequence.

Breathe in as you press the bar upward, and breathe out on the return movement.

43

STANDING SIDE (LATERAL) RAISE

For the muscles of the shoulders and upper back.

Assume an upright posture with feet approximately hip width apart. Hold a dumbbell in either hand, palms facing each other, just in front of the body, arms slightly bent at the elbows.

From this position, raise the dumbbells simultaneously to the side to reach a position just above head height, then lower under control to the starting position and repeat.

Avoid the tendency to throw the weights upward or lean forwards or backwards.

Breathe in as you raise your arms and out as you lower them.

SEATED ALTERNATE DUMBBELL PRESS

For the muscles of the shoulders, backs of upper arms and upper back.

Sit upright on a bench or sturdy chair. Place your feet apart and flat on the floor to give a firm, stable base. Have a dumbbell in each hand at shoulder level, palms facing inwards.

Smoothly press one dumbbell upward and overhead to arm's length, then control its movement back to the starting position, and repeat with the opposite arm. Keep your back straight throughout.

Breathe in as you raise each arm, and out as you lower.

45

UPRIGHT ROWING

For the muscles of the shoulders, upper back and biceps.

Stand tall holding a barbell, palms facing your body with your hands spaced approximately two thumbs' distance apart, with the bar at arm's length in front of your body.

From this position pull the bar upward to neck height making sure you keep your elbows high throughout. Lower the bar to the starting position under control and repeat the sequence.

Breathe in as you raise the bar, and out as you lower it.

Make sure the bar travels in a straight line as close as possible to your body.

PRESS ON BENCH

For the muscles of the chest, back of upper arm and front of shoulder.

Lie with your back flat on a bench, making sure your low back is pressed comfortably into the bench. You should maintain this position throughout the exercise.

Hold a barbell in the position at arm's length with a fairly wide grip. You will need the help of a partner for this.

Smoothly lower the bar so that it touches the middle of your chest then press it upwards to arm's length again.

Repeat the sequence.

Breathe out as you raise the bar, and in as you lower it.

47

DUMBBELL FLYES

For the muscles of the chest and front of shoulders.

Lie on a bench as in the previous exercise. This time hold a dumbbell in each hand, palms facing each other. Have your arms bent slightly at the elbow. The dumbbells should be positioned above your chest.

From this position take the arms out to the side under control as far as possible, then smoothly return to the starting position.

Breathe in as you lower your arms and out as you raise them.

PULLDOWN

For the muscles of the mid-upper back.

For this exercise you need to use a pulley, or pull-down machine.

If using a pulley, take a wide grip on the bar and kneel or sit in front of the weights stack with your arms at full length.

Smoothly pull the bar down so it touches the back of your neck. Hold this position momentarily, then smoothly control the movement back to the starting position.

Breathe out as you pull the bar down, and in on the return movement.

SINGLE ARM ROWING

For the muscles of the upper back and front of upper arm.

Start with your feet comfortably apart, bending forward from the waist using one hand to support yourself on a bench. Hold a dumbbell at arm's length in the other hand so that it is directly beneath the shoulder.

Smoothly bring the dumbbell up to the side of the chest and then control the movement back to the starting position. Repeat on both sides. Make sure to keep your back flat throughout.

Breathe in as you lift the dumbbell up and out as you return it.

To fully condition the abdominal muscles requires that you work in a number of different directions. One of the core exercises for abdominals in general is the curl up, lying on the floor.

CURL UP

Lie flat on the floor, with your knees bent at an angle, feet flat on the floor, low back pressed into the ground, arms by sides. This is the basic position you should start all abdominal work from. Breathe in. As you breathe out slowly, in a controlled manner raise your head and shoulders off the floor. Your back must be rounded throughout. The better the condition of your abdominal muscles the more of your body you will be able to peel off the floor, yet there is no great advantage to be gained by coming up any higher than the position illustrated.

Hold your final position momentarily, then slowly curl down and repeat the sequence.

Never allow your back to arch.

The exercise can be made more difficult by placing your hands across your chest and proceeding as before. The exercise is still more difficult with your hands behind your head.

DIAGONAL CURL UP

To work the diagonal muscles of the abdomen. Assume the basic curl up position, but come up leading with a twisting, curling up movement. Do this by placing one arm across the body and raising the shoulder of this arm just as in the illustration. Repeat the sequence on both sides breathing as before.

This exercise can also be made more difficult by placing the arms folded across the chest or behind the head.

There are many variations in abdominal exercises yet the basic rules outlined must be followed.

ALTERNATE KNEE TO ELBOW

Lie flat hands behind head, low back pressed into floor, knees slightly bent. Breathe in. As you breathe out, curl up twisting as you do so to bring your left elbow to your right knee. Curl down and repeat on the other side.

ABDOMINAL CRUNCH

Lie on floor with your legs supported on a chair or bench. Your knees should be above your hips and your hands behind your head. Breathe in. As you breathe out curl your head and shoulders towards your knees. Hold momentarily then return to the starting position, still keeping your low back pressed into the floor.

All the graded curl ups straight up and on the diagonal can also be advanced and carried out on an incline bench.

Do not go on to the incline until you can master the floor work.

SIDE BENDS
WITH A DUMBBELL

For the side abdominal muscles.

Stand tall with feet greater than shoulder width apart. Hold one dumbbell, palm facing your side and rest the other hand behind the back of your head. Keep the hips exactly where they are and bend to the side,

56

away from the dumbbell. Resist the tendency to lean either forward or backward and cultivate the feeling of lifting up and over to the side.

Breathe out as you bend, and in as you return.

Cool Downs *Stretches*

Towards the end of an exercise session all your muscles will be warm and will respond well to a stretching programme. A Cooling down phase including rhythmical movements and static stretches seems to prevent muscle soreness and aids exercise recovery. Never miss it out.

CAT STRETCH

Kneeling on all fours, round your back, breathing out as you do so.

Hold this position for a few seconds then arch your back, breathing in.

QUADRICEPS STRETCH

Stand tall, using a chair for support if necessary. Bend your leg at the knee to grasp your foot, bringing it towards your buttocks. Hold this position noting the stretch at the front of the thigh. Repeat on the other leg.

Breathe comfortably throughout.

SEATED STRETCH

Sit upright on the floor, legs straight out in front of you, feet flexed, backs of knees touching the floor. In this erect position, hinge forward from the hips keeping your back flat, and hold your final position.

Keep your chest lifted throughout.

Breathe easily throughout.

GROIN STRETCH

For the inside of the thighs.

Stand with feet spaced quite widely apart, hands on hips.

Turn the foot of the right leg to face the side: the foot of the left leg should face forward.

Move to the right by bending the knee of the right leg over the right foot, yet keeping the left leg straight and your upper body upright. Always make sure that the knee of the right leg moves in the same line as the foot.

You should feel a stretch along the inside of the left leg. Hold for a few seconds and repeat on each side.

Now return to the warm-up section and repeat exercises:

Arm circles

Hip circles

Waist twists

Side bends

Leg swings

with only half the number of repetitions. Then go for a slow jog or light easy cycle for 2-5 minutes, gradually moving more slowly to a near walking or stalling speed. Finish off by correcting your posture in front of a mirror, then take a cool refreshing shower.

Tony Lycholat is a qualified British Amateur Weight Lifting Association teacher and is also a British Amateur Athletics Board Coach. He has acted as a fitness adviser to exercise studios in London, and has devised many training programmes, including some for research into the effects of weight training at University College, London.

Thanks to the following for their help

Apple Dance and Fitness Centre
Grosvenor Road
Richmond
Surrey   (photography)

The Clifden Club
Richmond Adult College
The Clifden Centre
Twickenham   (additional weight training equipment)

Atlanta Sports Industries
Hooton Cliff Plantation
Hilltop
Hooton Roberts
South Yorkshire
            (photography and weight training equipment)

The Sweat Shop Ltd
The Causeway
Teddington
Middlesex
TW11 0HE   (clothing)

Reebok U.K. Ltd
26 St George's Quay
Lancaster   (footwear)